Koł
Sai-

WARNING

The techniques described in this book and the techniques of any martial art are dangerous. You have to train under the supervision of an expert. Please use caution when handling with any weapons and consult a qualified teacher. Please use restraint when practicing techniques described in this book. Neither the author nor the publishers of this book are responsible for the results of your choice to practice these techniques. Please respect the law and order of your country.

Helmut Kogel

KOBUDO SAI-JUTSU

Technique – Training – Kata

Meyer & Meyer Sport

British Library Cataloguing in Publication Data
A catalogue record for this book is available from the British Library

Kobudo – Sai-Jutsu
Helmut Kogel
Maidenhead: Meyer & Meyer Sport (UK) Ltd., 2009
ISBN: 978-1-84126-245-1

© 2009 by Meyer & Meyer Sport (UK) Ltd.
Aachen, Adelaide, Auckland, Budapest, Cape Town, Graz, Indianapolis,
Maidenhead, New York, Olten (CH), Singapore, Toronto
Member of the World
Sport Publishers' Association (WSPA)
www.w-s-p-a.org
Printed by: B.O.S.S Druck und Medien GmbH
ISBN: 978-1-84126-245-1
E-Mail: verlag@m-m-sports.com
www.m-m-sports.com

CONTENTS

PREFACE

This book on Sai-Jutsu can be seen as a supplement to the Bo-Jutsu book which has previously been released by the same publishing company. Sai-Jutsu originated on the island of Okinawa. The Sai weapon itself came to Okinawa by way of India and China. The refined Sai techniques, which were utilized as a defense against other weapons such a sword or spear, pay tribute to the painstaking creativity of the population of Okinawa and the outstanding Kobudo and Karate Masters of recent centuries. The island was overrun many times and at times occupied by hostile countries. This, combined with two governmental edicts forbidding the possession of weapons, led to development of a very special art of defense, which could be carried out with one's bare hands and everyday objects. The knowledge brought by Chinese martial arts Masters who either visited or lived on Okinawa was absorbed into the already existing martial arts there and resulted in significant further development of this martial arts system up to the present day.

This book is intended to provide the beginner with an introduction to the techniques of Sai-Jutsu, and also serve as an aid for advanced pupils and teachers in developing and consolidating their training. It provides an overview of the versatility of the Sai and the respective techniques ranging from beginner to advanced. Historical aspects have also been given their share of attention and, hopefully, will take the reader back in time to the era of the Kobudo pioneers. The knowledge I was able to gain in this area is basically due to the Grand Master Tetsuhiro Hokama from Okinawa, whom I thank for providing such abundant and excellent material.

As with the previously published Bo-Jutsu book, the Sai book also places its empha-sis on an illustrated presentation of basic and advanced techniques. Numerous graphic illustrations of traditional Katas (forms) will be a substantial help to the pupil, enabling him to absorb and learn new Katas or refine those he already knows. Experienced pupils are aware of how difficult it is to obtain teaching material for traditional Katas. It is extremely time-consuming to learn martial arts purely by watching video sequences, and the knowledge gained is often quickly forgotten. Mistakes creep in without being noticed and become a habit which is nearly always extremely difficult to erase. Unfortunately it was not common practice in earlier times to note down these Kobudo or Karate Katas either on Okinawa or in Japan, which means that a lot of knowledge has been lost and/or the traditional Katas themselves have been so changed deliberately or otherwise that they have assumed a completely different form.

Obviously this book is no replacement for quality training with a qualified teacher. It should, however, serve to provide the pupil with a more in-depth appreciation of the Sai as a weapon and also act as a guide for supplementary studies and training. It is my wish that this book motivates the reader to take an intensive interest in the Sai, and also that it help to preserve the cultural assets of Okinawa and of Japan.

Lippstadt, Germany, 11-24-2007

H. Kogel, MD, Professor of Surgery

5th Dan Shotokan Karate Renshi (IMAF Kokusai Budoin)
5th Dan Kobudo
2nd Dan Nihon Jujutsu
1st Antas Combat Arnis

INTRODUCTION

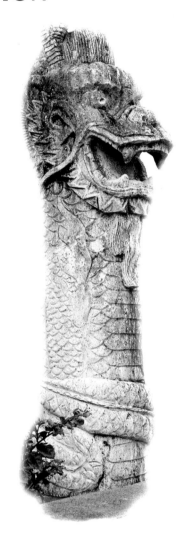

Among all known Ways you may also find the Way to salvation through the teachings of Buddha, while others follow the Confucian Way of learning, the doctor values all means of healing sickness, the poet on the other hand teaches the Way of the Waka-poem, or perhaps we can speak of a follower of the tea or the bow and arrow; whichever art, whichever talent, each is eagerly practiced, people feel themselves drawn to them, to belong. Only a few are drawn to the Way of the martial arts.

Miyamoto Musashi, A Book of Five Rings

INTRODUCTION

T he Sai is the traditional weapon associated with Kubu Jutsu, Okinawa's Art of Weaponry. Kubu Jutsu (pronounced Kobu Jitsu) was later renamed Kobudo following the philosophical changes which took place in Japanese martial arts during the 1950s. The Sai is also to be found in other countries such as China and India. Knowledge of the Sai is imperative for Karate and other related martial arts when aiming to improve non-armed techniques carried out with the bare hand. This relatively small weapon never fails to impress with its versatility. Several excellent books and videos have already been released by various authors dealing with how to handle the Sai, and these have helped contribute to the spread of what is, indeed, an interesting Okinawa weapon. The various Katas, however, have to date not received sufficient atten-

Sai Jutsu, Calligraphy by Tetsuhiro Hokama

tion in previous publications. All those who practice the martial arts have at some stage come up against the following problem: no sooner have you been introduced to a wonderful new Kata during a seminar or course, or coached by a Master, only to return home and find you are unable to carry out exactly what you have just been taught despite your sometimes numerous written notes and sketches. Or, the Master tries to penetrate further into the Kata during a follow-up seminar and his pupil is unable to follow him because he is still too preoccupied with the actual surface of execution itself. In Shotokan Karate these days you will find many excellent Kata diagrams which provide for easier lead-up and execution. Albrecht Pflueger was a pioneer in approaching this problem many years ago, with his excellent graphic illustrations. With a few exceptions, however, this manner of clear graphic Kata representation is sadly missing in other Karate styles, and the same applies to the Art of Weaponry in Kobudo. Graphic illustrations are available for all too few Katas and weapons although exactly that is what is needed to provide support in carrying them through and making it much easier to work with them.

For this reason we have included graphic presentations of six traditional Sai Katas from Okinawa in this book, as we also did in the Bo-Jutsu book previously released by the same publishing company. Practicing with the Sai, in particular, provides an excellent opportunity to refine and optimize technical flow. This book can obviously not take the place of training with an experienced teacher, nor can it replace the need for intensive seminar work with the weapon. Rather, it should function as a welcome addition to the knowledge and information which can otherwise only be attained through personal contact, and should assist in progressing from a surface to in-depth appreciation of the martial arts – to use a simile, seeing the outer surface of a jug does not satisfy our curiosity – we want to know what's in it and what secrets it might contain. With this book we are aiming to open the reader's mind for this impressive traditional Okinawan weapon and provide an additional stimulus for those who already have some prior experience. An additional aim was to provide a few historical insights into the development of the Okinawa Kobudo and, thanks to the generosity of Dr. Tetsuhiro Hokama (an expert in the field of Karate history and Grand Master of Okinawa) we were able to include in the book several of his calligraphies and historical photos. Dr. Tetsuhiro Hokama is 10th Dan Karate, Kobudo, Kyusho, Hanshi. Finally, we need to impress upon the reader that the Sai is also a dangerous weapon which, when not treated with due care, can result in injury to both the user and others. We stress that its use should be learned solely under the supervision of an experienced expert and that, last but not least, the respective laws of your country must be adhered to.

January 2007 in Dojo from Sensei Tetsuhiro Hokama in Nishihara, Okinawa

ACKNOWLEDGMENTS

This book would not have been possible without the unstinting support of many teachers, friends and numerous helpers. My interest in Kobudo was awakened roughly 15 years ago by my friend and teacher of many years, Hans Dieter Rauscher (8th Dan Hanshi, 6th Dan Kobudo Kyoshi, 7th Dan Iaido Kyoshi etc.) after having been actively occupied with Karate and Jujutsu since 1973. Through him and the IMAF Kokusai Budoin (International Martial Arts Federation) I came into contact with further experts such as Ikio Higushi (9th Dan Shotokan Karate, Gimma Ryu, Hanshi und 7th Dan Kobudo Kyoshi) and Kazuo Sakai (10th Dan Wado Ryu Karate, Kobudo, Hanshi), and was fortunate enough to learn and train first-hand on several occasions under these Japanese Grand Masters. My particular thanks and appreciation, therefore, to Hans Dieter Rauscher, Ikio Higushi and Kazuo Sakai. Thank you, also, to Shizuya Sato (10th Dan Nihon Jujutsu, 9th Dan Judo, Chief Director of the IMAF) for his support and also for instructing me in Nihon Jujutsu. Several years ago I happened to meet Dr. Tetsuhiro Hokama while visiting Okinawa on business. It was through him that I was able to gain a deeper insight into the practice and the history of Okinawa's martial arts. Hokama (10th Dan Karate, Kobudo, Kyusho, Hanshi) introduced me to a type of Karate and Kobudo which can only be described as unusual. Many of the illustrations and numerous calligraphies which you will find in this book were made available by him. Together with him I was able to carry out studies on Kyusho Jutsu, which have been documented in two as yet unpublished books. During his first seminar in Germany, which took place in Endingen in March 2007, he was able to establish his concept of Karate and Kobudo as being valuable in the eyes of many international martial arts experts. My thanks, also, to my sons Lutz and Marc. It was my good fortune that both of my sons shared my enthusiasm for Japanese martial arts from their childhood and have continuously given me their active and unfailing support. Thank you to my wife Elvira for the patience she has shown, especially during and despite my frequent absence, and also for her assistance with the photo sessions. Thanks also to Ms. Judy Keenan for the excellent translation of the book from German to English language. And finally, thanks to the employees of Meyer and Meyer Sport, Mr. Stengel, Ms. Deutz and Ms. Reinders for their active support with this, my second book. Publishing this book in such an impressive form would not have been possible without their excellent active participation and help.

Calligraphy by Tetsuhiro Hokama, Katsu (Kyusho, give Energy)

A GENERAL PART:
HISTORY AND BACKGROUND

1 **The Origin of the Sai**
2 **Okinawa's Kobudo Masters**
3 **Anatomy of the Sai**
4 **Movement Theory**
5 **Basic Tactical Principles**
6 **Basic Rules**

    Holds (Mochi)

    Etiquette (Re, Yoi, Hajime, Naore)

1. THE ORIGIN OF THE SAI

The following rule applies when evaluating the meaning of a weapon:
The use of every weapon is dependent upon circumstance, it happens at the
appropriate moment in time.

Miyamoto Musashi, A Book of Five Rings

THE ORIGIN OF THE SAI

The origin of the Sai has not been entirely established beyond doubt. What we know from Manji Sai and from Jitte (Jutte) suggests that Okinawa's fishermen used it as a tool e.g. to haul in fish. The idea of the trident having been used by farmers to draw or mark out furrows in their fields is nothing more than speculation as the Sai would have been quite unsuitable for this type of work. Tridents with either a short or a long shaft have repeatedly occurred in several cultures. Poseidon, for example, the God of the Sea in Greek mythology, is pictured with a long-shafted trident. A similar implement crops up in German mythology as a thunderhead and the Devil is often shown with a trident in his hand. The occurrence of similar symbols suggests that the origins lay somewhere between Euphrates, Tigris and the Nile Delta, which means it could even go back to the origins of human civilization.

Dr. Dr. h. c. Tetsuhiro Hokama, a Karate Grand Master from Okinawa and cultural historian, believes that the origins of the martial arts also go back as far as Mesopotamia and that past mass migration spread them via India to China and Japan. This also applies to the art of acupuncture, which we tend to attribute to the Chinese. Older findings point at countries such as India and Europe, although any definitive knowledge in these countries has unfortunately been lost over the years. In India one can find the Trishul (trident) which we connect with the Hindu God Shiva, and which Hokama considers to be the origin of the Okinawa Sai. The Indian Trishul symbolizes three functions: creation, protection and destruction. With a long shaft it is known as Khtavanga. According to Hindu belief the three ends contain Sat (truth), Chit (awareness) and Ananda (emotions). Older information on other cultures indicates that the longer prong of the trident could stand for the present, with the two shorter prongs meaning the past and the future. The Sai is a typical Okinawa weapon which only appears in Japan at a later date. It was used as a defense against various other weapons such as the Bo and the sword. It has the advantage of being versatile, made of metal and being able to hook into or stop an opposing weapon. Its direct use against the human body allows devastating combinations of attack aimed at the destruction of joints, blood vessels and nerves. It can be used as a purely defensive weapon designed to warn and fend off an opponent, or as a utensil which allows absolute finality against dangerous weapons such as a sword, in order to save one's own life. The tradition of the Sai is as old on Okinawa as are Kobudo and Karate. It is impossible to separate one from the other. Families and schools (Ryua) have occupied themselves with it since the 14th century, developing it further and passing it on. Elements of the Chinese Kempo and the Quan Fa melted into the old Okinawan art of Okinawa Ti at the same time as there was a blending of Chinese and Okinawan art of weaponry. The various bans on weapons in Okinawa in the 15th century led to a more intensive development of these arts using everyday utensils (Bo, Kama, Sai, Tinbe, Oar, Tonfa, Tekko and many others). The art of Sai Jutsu is reflected in many traditional Katas which can be attributed to varying eras and differing Kobudo schools. This book contains a selection of Katas originating from several of those eras and schools.

Sai, Calligraphy by T. Hokama

2. OKINAWA'S KOBUDO MASTERS

The following list is an introduction to several Okinawan Kobudo Masters with the intention of providing more insight into the interwoven nature of Okinawa's Schools of Karate and Kobudo. At this point I would like to express once again my special thanks to Dr. Tetsuhiro Hokama, who painstakingly compiled a great deal of historical material out of his books, which he then made available to me. The literary index also lists other authors such as Werner Lind, who has been actively involved in intensive research in these fields and without whom we would only have a fraction of the knowledge we now have. Even today the majority of Okinawa's Masters practice Karate as well as Kobudo. The entire martial arts system also includes Tuite (techniques for joint manipulation comparable to the Chinese Chin Na), Kyusho (attacks directed against sensitive vital points) and a series of throws. These various elements have been more or less completely passed down in Okinawa for generations.

The varying weapons systems originate partially from neighboring Asian countries such as India, China and the Philippines; they were then combined with Okinawa's own weapons techniques and developed further. The election of suitable techniques simply followed the rule of practicality. Effective techniques were retained, impractical techniques were rejected. The various weapons bans which came into place in Okinawa during the reign of Lord Shi Shin (1501) and during the Satsuma Dynasty (around 1609) played an important role in speeding up the development of Karate and other fighting techniques among the Okinawa population. Everyday items such as

Kobu Jutsu, Calligraphy by Tetsuhiro Hokama

oars, flails and stirrups, for example, had to function as weapons born of necessity. An iron-ore deficit and the ensuing ban on weapons made of iron led specifically to further development of wooden weapons on the Ryu Kyu islands. The population became more and more intensely involved with martial arts as a necessary means of self-defense against attack and the prevailing despotism of the generally disliked and unwelcome occupying forces. They trained in secret (discovery would have meant punishment) and disguised their fighting techniques as folk dancing, so called Odoris, which still exist today. (Similar dances can be found in other countries, e.g. Korea.) This meant that over a period of time there was a chance for many specialists to develop in differing Okinawan weapon disciplines, some of them achieving fame well beyond their own regional borders. Ongoing cultural and trade exchange with China also brought further contact with martial arts experts from that country, this in turn continuing to enrich and develop the special philosophy and martial arts of Okinawan. These also included government officials (Sappushi) of the Chinese Emperor. The first Chinese immigrants arrived in 1393 (envoys, public servants, teachers, commercial traders) and settled in the vicinity of the Naha harbor in Kumemura. They introduced Okinawa to Chinese culture, Chinese medicine and Chinese martial arts and were a substantial part of the island's administrative development. One of these was Ambassador Kusanku (Ko Shu Kun), a key figure in martial arts who passed his knowledge on to the Masters of the Okinawa Te (an old Okinawa martial art of fist fighting).

Sakugawa Peichin Kanga

(1733-1815, 1762-1843 or 1782-1837)
The recorded details of his life are not all that specific. He was born in Akata in Shuri under the name of Teruya Kanga. He changed his name after being awarded the Chikudon Peichin for Higher Service. He is reputed to have studied under the monk Takahara Peichin, as well as under various Chinese martial arts masters. In Kume he made the acquaintance of the Chinese Envoy and martial arts expert Kusanku (Ko Shu Kun), through whom he was among other things later initiated into the Kata Kushanku (later Kanku Dai). He was a teacher at the Government School (Kogugaku) of the Kingdom of Ryu Kyu. The famous Bujutsu School Sakugawa no Kon is accredited to him, as is the Kata which carries the same name. He is believed to have travelled to Peking on five occasions and came into contact there with Quan Fa. He became nationally known as Tôde (China Fist) Sakugawa and founded the basis for the Shuri Te. According to records he died in Peking in 1837. His student Matsumura Sokon (whom he taught at the age of 78) is supposed to have discovered his remains in a cemetery outside Peking and returned them to Okinawa. Another of his students Matsumora Kosaku (1829-1898), a well-known Tomari Te Master, was a powerful fighter with a straightforward character. He joined forces with other inhabitants of his hometown Tomari to protect them from foreign invaders such as the Satsuma.

Tomb of Matsumora Kosaku on Okinawa

Chatan Yara

(1740-1812)
Chatan Yara probably came from Shuri. He was a well-known Kobujutsu expert during the reign of King Sho Boku on Ryu Kyu. He lived in Chatan and passed down the famous Sai Kata Chatan Yara no Sai, as well as the Kata Chatan Yara no Kusanku. He studied the Kata Kusanku, as did Sakugawa, under the tutorship of the Chinese Envoy Kwan Chang Fu (Kosokun – there are various written versions, see above). This Kata was then passed on to Kyan Chotoku, Arakaki and Shimabuku Taro.

Matsumura Sokon

(1800-1892, 1798-1890 or 1809-1896)
Matsumura was born in Yamakawa in Shuri. Once again there are no exact records to be had. He was known under the names Bucho or Unyo, his Chinese name being Wu Chengda. He had a relationship with Tsuru, a woman who was also highly competent in the martial arts and who is supposed to have developed the Kata Hangetsu. Matsumura learned the so-called Jigen Ryu, a Japanese sword fighting art, from Satsuma, which he then passed on to several students such as Asato Anko

(one of Gichin Funakoshi's teachers) and Tarashiki Chochu. This became the origin of the Tsuken Bo Kata, which then passed on to Tsuken Uekata Sesoku from Shuri and other students. Another stream is believed to have been passed on through Bushi Tsuken Hantagwa over Nakamura Kame, Tamagusuku, Akachu, Komesu to Soken Hohan. Matsumura established important rules in Karate, these being: flowing movement, giving way to achieve victory, the 7 wisdoms of Karate. He often travelled to China and, in the vicinity of Fouzhou studied Shaolin Kempo and the Art of Weaponry, after which he founded his own particular style, the Shorin-Ryu (i.e. Shaolin Ryu). He was later placed in charge of the Royal Guard of the Ryu Kyu king. He brought with him from China a copy of the "Bubishi," a document about the Chinese martial arts which had long been kept secret. While a copy of this was preserved by Chinese families in Kume, the original is currently believed to be somewhere in Taiwan (information handed down by word of mouth).

Earlier storage place of the "Bubishi" in Kume-Shizeibyo

He came into contact with the martial arts Master Iwah in China, who taught him the secret techniques of the Crane Style and the Kata Hakatsuru.

Matsumura Sokon Memorial near Shuri, Okinawa

Shinko Matayoshi

(1888-1947)

Shinko Matayoshi was born in Kakinohana in Naha. He learned how to use weapons such as the Bo, Eku and Sai as a youth, under the tutorage of Higa Gusshikawa Tairagawa. In addition he learned how to use the Tonfa and Nunchaku from Ire of Nosato, Chatan. Towards the end of the Meijin era he lived with bandits in Manchuria, where he learned to ride and to use the bow and arrow, as well as how to handle a lasso. He later went to Shanghai and studied the use of other weapons as well as Chinese medicine, acupuncture and moxibustion. It was here that he came into contact with the Crane Style of the Shaolin Qan (Hakutsuru-Ken). He returned to Okinawa in 1935 as a renowned weapons expert and actively helped to spread Kobudo by joining Gichi Funakoshi to take part in public demonstrations of martial arts on Okinawa, in Tokyo, Osaka and Kyoto. His son Shinpo Matayoshi has carried on the tradition and continued his work and thirst for knowledge.

Shinpo Matayoshi

(1921-1997)

Shinpo Matayoshi was born in Kina, the city of Yomitan on Okinawa. As Shinko Matayoshi's son, he started his training at the early age of 7. He studied Shorin Ryu Karate under the famous Master Kyan Chotoku and learned Shaolin boxing which originated in the south from Go Kenki. He became known both nationally and internationally as a distinguished Kobudo expert, as was his father, and in 1971 founded the All Okinawa Kobudo Federation. For a long time he trained in the Dojo of

Seiko Higa (1898-1966) together with Tetsuhiro Hokama, with whom he maintained a close friendship until his death on September 7, 1997.

Matayoshi Shinpo and Tetsuhiro Hokama during a New Year Celebration in Naha

Taira Shinken

(1897-1970)
His original family name was Maezato, which he used to name several of his Katas, such as Maezato no Tekko (among others). He studied Karate under Gichin Funakoshi and Yabiku Moden. He became actively involved in trying to reactivate the art of Kobudo which, at that time, was being pushed into the background on Okinawa by Karate. He taught both Karate and Kobudo in various Dojos on Okinawa and on the main Japanese island and, in 1955, founded a society for the preservation and further support of Ryu Kyu Kobudo. He set down the first books on the Art of Weaponry and played an important and decisive role in its promotion not only in Japan but worldwide. In 1960 he was appointed Shihan of the Nihon Kobudo Kenkyujo. He functioned as a higher dignitary in many Karate and Kobudo societies. His students included well-known masters such as Akamine Eisuke (1925-1999), Motokatsu Inoue (1918-1993), Hayashi Teruo (1926-2004), Mabuni Kenwa (1889-1952) and many others.

Soken Hohan

(1891-1982)
Soken Hohan was born in Nishihara on Okinawa and studied under his uncle Matsumura Nabe, who in turn was a grandchild of the famous Bushi Matsumura Sokon. He was considered to be a significant Kyusho expert (among other things George Dillman's trainer) and at an early age learned Sai Jutsu and Kama Jutsu. He learned Bo Jutsu and Nunchaku from Tsuken Akachu and was instructed in Tonfa Jutsu by Master Kobahigawa. He had many students who later achieved significant standing and became well-known. He represented the direct school descending from Matsumura Sokon and was trained in the secret Crane Style by his uncle, Kata Hakutsuru.

Tetsuhiro Hokama

Tetsuhiro Hokama was born in 1944 in Taiwan. He began his training in Karate and Bo under his grandfather, Seiken Tokuyama, who studied under Oshiro Chojo (1888-1935). It was Oshiro who created the famous Bo Kata Oshiro no Kun (also known as Ufugusuku no Kun). Hokama trained further under Seiko Higa (1898-1966), who had in turn studied directly under Higaonna Kanryo (1853-1915) and Chojun Miyagi (1888-1953). Following Higa's death, Hokama continued his training under Higa's top student Fukushi Seiko (1919-1975). In Seiko Higa's Dojo Hokama came into contact with Shinpo Matayoshi, under whose tutorage he deepened his studies in Kobudo. Hokama was also able to learn the secret techniques of the Hakatsuru-Ken (Crane Style). He came from a family steeped in tradition, which had been involved in the martial arts for generations. His family tree is large and goes back a long way. One of his ancestors was Hokama (Yabu) Peichin (around 1644) who actively practiced the martial arts. Yet another ancestor was a royal guard to the Chinese Emperor. In Japan Hokama is considered to be one of the most honored of the Okinawan Masters and is President of the Goju Ryu Kenshikai Karate Kobudo Association and Curator of the Karate Museum in Nishihara Okinawa, which he founded. He is active in researching the history of Karate, as a result of which he has been honored with academic titles by two foreign universities. He is also an excellent master of calligraphy. The name Hokama stands for a very dynamic style of Karate and Kobudo. The combination of the typical elements of Goju Ryu Karate (Go – hard and Yu – soft) can be clearly seen and the typical Goju Ryu principles are reflected in his Kobudo.

A youthful Tetsuhiro Hokama with Shinpo Matayoshi in Seiko Higa's Dojo around 1963

3. ANATOMY OF THE SAI

Constant practice, from the early through to the late hours, of the prescribed road to the martial arts according to my school will automatically lead to greater composure.

Miyamoto Musashi, A Book of Five Rings

ANATOMY OF THE SAI

The Sai comes in various forms, as can be seen in the illustrations below. The Manjii Sai, mounted on a long stick, is called Nunti Bo. There are many uses and Katas for these weapons. The Nunti Bo is a typical fisherman's tool, used to haul fish on board or to draw in another boat.

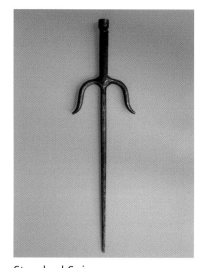

Standard Sai

Manji (Matayoshi) Sai

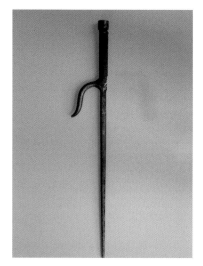

Jutte (Jitte)

The anatomy of the Sai can be roughly compared with the human anatomy, as illustrated, which makes it easier to comprehend its use as a weapon.

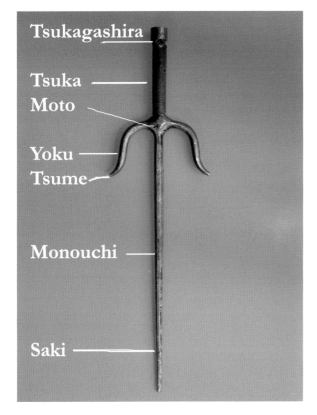

Tsukagashira

Tsuka
Moto

Yoku
Tsume

Monouchi

Saki

The Sai has great versatility, as it can used with its main spear (Saki), the shaft (Monouchi), the knob (Tsukugashira) and the barbs on the side (Tsume). This makes it unpredictable in conflict. Technically seen it allows for striking, jabbing, diverting and cutting. The same principle applies to the Sai as to Karate: every tactic for defense should be a simultaneous attack. Every defense should mean not only an attack on the opponent's weapon but also against the opponent (e.g. the hands). Considering that the human body has more than 350 vital points, this allows for an enormous variety of vulnerable areas.

4. MOVEMENT THEORY

The stances for the five directions are these: the upper, the middle, the lower, to the left and to the right... The middle stance can be seen as the General, the four remaining positions are subordinate to the General. This principle must always be taken into consideration.

Miyamoto Musashi, A Book of Five Rings

TRAINING MOVEMENT

Generally speaking, the most important element in all martial arts is movement control and a feeling for whichever natural movement is tactically suited to the given situation. This includes the elements of distance (Mai), utilizing direction (angle) to deflect force (Tai Sabaki) and utilization of your own acceleration through retracting or drawing back your hand(s) and hips (Hikite). One of the basic elements of Kobudo is that the body and the weapon are one entity (ken-tai-ichi-jo). This requires not only that each movement be powerful and exact, but also that movement combinations need to differ in detail according to the type of weapon used, even the length of the stick used. On the surface it would be easy to fall into the trap of believing this not to be particularly difficult, however we must remember that a feeling for movement means being in control of all three spatial dimensions (height, length and depth). In a time in which the computer has become more and more overwhelmingly present in the everyday life of our children and youth, it is becoming ever clearer that this feeling for spatial dimensions is diminishing and being replaced by a two-dimensional world. This is obvious over and over again when young people in a test situation have difficulty in confidently moving backwards. Every Karate pupil and teacher has experienced the phenomenon that a backwards movement often results in a loss of coordination. Simple combinations which can be carried out without difficulty in a forward direction suddenly do not function when moving backwards. It requires a good deal of training to overcome these coordination problems and it is one of the basic principles of Karate that combinations and techniques automatically be out carried in every direction without having to think about it. Coordination problems become particularly obvious in free-style fighting. Students are often not quick enough to dodge or retreat when the opponent attacks, making defense or counterattacks appear clumsy and ineffective. The importance of the time-factor for spatial movement also tends to be forgotten all too often. Timing and speed play a decisive role in the success of the techniques used. Even when an opposing attack is hard and effective, it is still possible to win sufficient time to launch a counterattack by changing your angle and instigating a defense movement, however weak (e.g. Nagashi Uke). This means it is important for the trainer to incorporate the factor of time in movement training and fight tactics.

DEGREES of freedom of movement

In principle we have the ability to move forwards, backwards and sideways. But that is leaving out the dimension of height, which was described as a possible direction of movement by a famous Japanese sword fighter, Miyamoto Musashi (1584-1645) in his Book of the Five Rings. One example of this is tactical evasion by ducking. In the interests of simplicity only a few diagrams have been used when drawing various lines on the floor to illustrate possible movement direction in defense or attack.

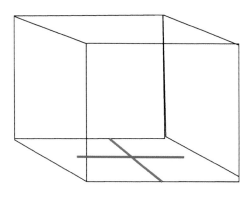

Graphic 1

The simplest diagram shows the directions forwards and backwards, left and right sideways at a 90° angle.

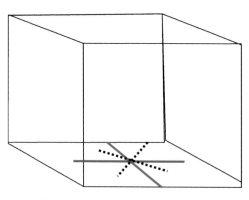

Graphic 2

A further development of this diagram is one that includes the 45° angles.

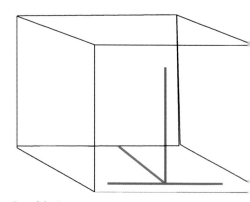

Graphic 3

Musashi's diagram includes height and only shows flat directions forwards and backward as well as sideways to the left and the right.

In Kobudo the 45° movement is basically theoretical, more so than in Karate. In practice you find that angle modification in sideways movement is fluid and not clearly defined. It is the distance to the opponent which defines angle and, accordingly, direction of movement. The decisive point is achieving the correct distance (Mai) to allow the optimum use of one or the other technique. The particular difficulty in Kobudo lies in melting together with the weapon you are using and thus achieving an inner feeling for the correct distance. The Sai can be used short or long, meaning that it requires constant adjustment of distance, swinging and dodging, which is typical for the Sai. This creates suppleness and speed, two elements which are absolutely necessary for working with the Sai.

The importance of these principles seem obvious. If someone happens to be aiming an axe or a sword at your forehead, it is useless to try to deflect the blow with a Jodan Hiraki Uke (double upwards block), even if you were using a Sai made of iron. The force of the blow is so great that your own head would be hit. Retreat is pointless, as the opponent is generally faster and more defined in his forward movement and can continue to attack with undiminished force. The only remaining chance is to alter the distance and the angle by turning the body (Tai Sabaki). This allows you to escape the focus of the attack, to deflect and diminish its force. These factors also play a role in the chapter dealing with tactics. Force cannot always be countered or neutralized with the same amount of force. In most cases it is more effective to dodge and parry. Harmony in combining two opposites (Go – hard, and Ju – dodge at the right moment) is what leads to success. Movements from a 45° angle are decisive in practicing the martial arts successfully. This is the easiest way of carrying out simultaneous actions of attack and defense, and is at the same time the very principle of Tai Sabaki. The 45° angle is also often the key to a successful hit. In Kyusho Jutsu (martial arts incorporating attack against vital body parts) we find that importance is placed on hitting a sensitive nerve (e.g. point of acupuncture) at a 45° angle. The meridian nerve structures react the same way as piezoelectrical elements, in that they can only be optimally aroused or lamed when touched at a certain angle.

"There is nothing in this world which exists which is softer and thinner than water. And yet there is nothing comparable when overcoming that which is hard and rigid.
We all know that weakness can defeat strength, that hardness can be conquered by the soft, and yet none of us acts accordingly."
Laotse

Once again we are faced with a principle which is eminently suited to use in every-day life. To sum it up we can say that the foregoing principles of movement theory are the necessary basis for correct application of counter techniques, attack and/or a throw. The right approach to technique is the key to success. I have combined this with the factor of time to lead us into another chapter which can be described as basic tactical principles. The use of a weapon (in this case the Sai) makes it more difficult to use a movement diagram to find the correct distance (Mai). The efficiency of a particular technique is, however, dependent on exactly that, as an incorrect focus results in loss of effect. Considering all of these points it is easier to understand that it is more difficult to correctly use the Sai than we have experienced from weaponless Karate techniques or other disciplines. Constant training is the decisive basis.

Using the Hips

Correct use of the hips is of utmost importance for mastering effective and fast techniques with the Sai. Using the hips is the key to learning the correct technique, much more so than with any other weapon. Without it the techniques become static and ineffective. A student who has learned to handle the Sai correctly can then go on to further develop his Karate, which is what makes the Sai in Kobudo an important supplementary element to Karate. Movements and stances in Okinawan Kobudo differ from the Karate of the main island. The stances are higher, to enable faster action. Some stances are differently named. Movements are dictated by the weapon and are extremely fast and dynamic. Age Uke and Gedan Barai are placed to a more outward position, to provide better protection to the lower arm, from which Karate also profits as it is easier on the bones (ulna and radius).

5. BASIC TACTICAL PRINCIPLES

The following rule can be applied when evaluating the fighting area: the sun is to be carried on your shoulders...
The first of three possibilities is known as Ken-no-Sen, which means: anticipating your opponent in that attack (Ken) arises from your initiative (Sen). A second possibility is called Tai-no-Sen, which means: while awaiting (Tai) your opponent's attack, take the initiative (Sen). The third possibility is Taitai-no-Sen, which means: when both sides are equal (Taitai), take the initiative (Sen).
These are the three alternatives. There is no other way to begin, regardless of the conflict.

Miyamoto Musashi, A Book of Five Rings

BASIC TACTICAL PRINCIPLES

Zanshin

A vital element of the martial arts is constant readiness for conflict and utmost concentration even in phases in which no obvious action is taking place. This serves to ensure that one is not taken by surprise and overwhelmed by an unexpected attack. An important requirement is not to lose visual contact and not to be distracted by unimportant visual details. In Laido (sword fighting) the gaze is directed through the opponent to an imaginary point approximately 6 m further on. This enables you to maintain a general overview and react quickly even when faced with several opponents. Using the same principle, it would be incorrect to focus on the opponent's weapon in Kobudo as it is not the weapon itself which initiates the attack, but the opponent who is holding the weapon. An opponent's body language announces the start of an attack much earlier than can be seen in the movement of his weapon. Focusing on the weapon will mean that it is then already too late to react. The faster the weapon, the more important the tactical rule, which particularly applies to the short stick, knives and Nunchaku. No one waits for a pistol to be fired before trying to avoid the shot – it is more advisable to take cover beforehand. Making and maintaining eye contact is important when attempting to psychologically gain the upper hand against an opponent. If you look at the floor you have already lost. Readiness to fight, however, does not necessarily mean bodily tension as this would result in too slow a start. You need to move loosely and freely to take advantage of starting at exactly the right moment and landing a hit. Maximum tension (Kime) is built up only for the end phase of the strike.

Sen no Sen

There are various alternatives for correct defensive timing when attacked. One of these is the principle of Sen no Sen, which entails anticipating your opponent before he has completed his attacking move. Its possibilities include not only making a faster start than your opponent at the moment he begins his attack, but also in changing your angle so that he meets nothing but thin air, or to dodge and escape the focus of the attack, enabling you to then land your own attack faster. This is a typical method of attack in Karate and Laido and is a widely accepted principle.

Go no Sen

This refers to attack rising out of defense. It means dodging when under attack, using a light defensive movement, and then immediately starting through in your own offensive. It is a particularly effective tactic when your opponent is attacking strongly, as a trial of strength has fewer advantages than following the principle of evasion. Drawing an imaginary line, Sen no Sen represents forwards movement whereas Go no Sen is retreat followed by a classic forwards movement (swing out and then in).

Tai Sabaki

Tai Sabaki involves turning your body to avoid an attack and at the same time adopting a more advantageous position for your own attack. It is a typical basic tactical principle which is often used in Aikido. At the same time it also means maintaining your own balance to cause your opponent to fall, so that he can be easily overwhelmed. Changing the angle of attack results in your opponent's attack being weakened and allows you to gain a superior start position. The direction of movement is always sideways. Usually these movements offer the best chance for a throw, as in Judo. This type of movement is especially fast and effective with a weapon, particularly when attacking with a long stick. The 45° angle is the key, as it is usually very effective and also successful in Kyusho.

Debana o Kujiku

Debana Waza is a form of surprise attack. Debana o Kujiku means "distracting and overwhelming your opponent by a surprise attack." The effect is dependent on exact timing of the initiative for starting your first attack. It can be difficult, however it is an important tactic when your opponent is physically superior or when he has a superior weapon.

The various tactical principles described here represent the largest section of possible action, although there are many other variations.
Handling the Sai requires a special feeling for fighting with weapons in general. It is useless when going into defense against weapons such as the Bo, for example, to concentrate on stopping or deflecting the weapon. This is not the true tactical principle of Okinawa's martial arts. The weapon itself (e.g. the Bo) does not present the danger, but rather the opponent using it. In other words, you have to defend

yourself against the wielder of the weapon. You have to go into attack, and to do that you need to concentrate on the part of the body nearest to you, which is mostly the opponent's foremost hand. If you are able to land a blow here, your opponent is no longer completely capable of handling his weapon (examples are given in the chapters „Basic Techniques I" (p. 80-81) and „Basic Kumite with Partner" (p. 98-107). Focus is placed on further blows to particularly sensitive body parts, such as the vital points of the body (Kyusho). In earlier times this was one way of ending a fight quickly and without dangerous injuries.

"A clever tactician can be compared with the Shuairan. The Shuairan is a snake found in the Chang mountains. If you strike a blow to its head, it will attack you with its tail; if you attack the tail, you will be attacked by its head. If you strike a blow to its mid-section, it will attack with both its head and its tail."
SUNZI, the Art of War

6. BASIC RULES

When teaching the martial arts, I start by giving the student who has begun this journey those principles which he can easily and quickly comprehend, according to his talent.

Miyamoto Musashi, A Book of Five Rings

BASIC RULES

Holding the Sai (Mochi)

Etiquette
- Bow (Re)
- Prepare (Yoi)
- Start Position (Hajime)
- Separating (Naore)
- Finishing (Bow)

HOLDING THE SAI (MOCHI)

There are various ways of holding the Sai. Its very versatility arises out of skilled, fast changes of hold which allow it to be used at differing distances. This makes it difficult to exactly anticipate a Sai attack.

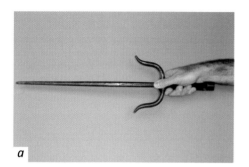

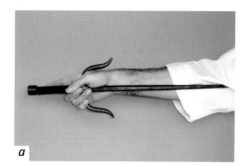

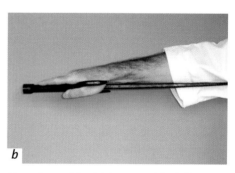

Honte Mochi (natural hold)

Gyuakute Mochi (reversed hold)

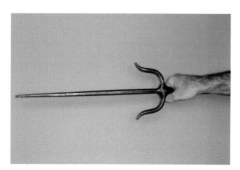

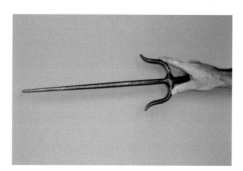

Ippon Honte

Yoku Honte

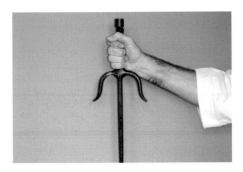

Tsuka Honte

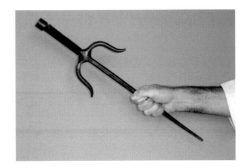

Gyakute Toku

Honte Toku

There are, of course, many other holds which are of no particular practical importance, such as Ippon Honte, Honte Toku, Gyakute Yoku etc.

The thumb changes its position when handling the Sai (see below). A firm fist hold is an absolute necessity for controlling the Sai. Acceleration comes from the hips and wrists, whereby the shoulder only plays a minor role. The small finger is a crucial factor to manual power and for locking in the techniques. Take particular care to avoid self-injury when handling the Sai. The prong is

not meant to bore through one's own ribs, which is why – other than in Karate – the rear fist should be rotated by 90° only and not 180°.

Hold Change (Mochikake)

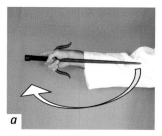
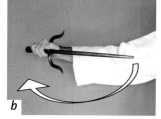
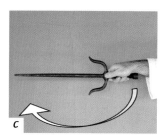

Horizontal Flip I

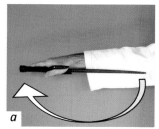

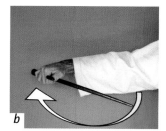
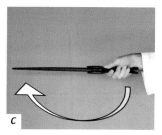

Horizontal Flip II

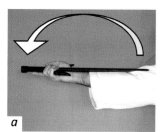

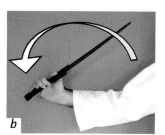
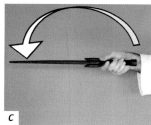

Vertical Flip

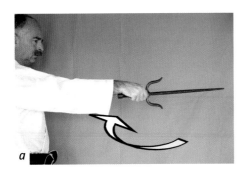

Kaeshi Uchi Wrist Rotation Strike from outer position

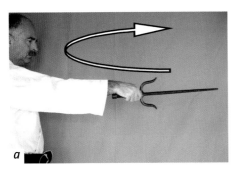

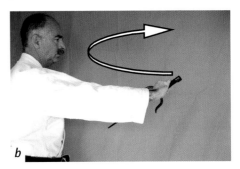

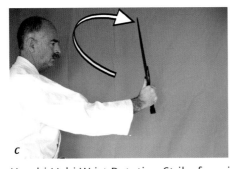

Kaeshi Uchi Wrist Rotation Strike from inner position

Being able to use the Sai correctly means being able to take advantage of its weight to achieve acceleration. This results in the typical snapping movements of the Sai. The Sai snap-back is called Omote and constitutes the major part of fast hold and technique changes. It is practiced again and again in the Katas. The Sai has specific characteristics which enable it to be used for jabs, strikes, thrusts, deflection and locked hooking. Some Sais also have sharp blades so that the weapon can also be used for cutting. There are certain similarities between the Sai in Kobudo and the hand in Karate. Gyakute Mochi (inner hold) can be compared to fist techniques. Honte Mochi (outer hold) resembles the sword hand (Nukite) in Karate. Some Katas are carried out with three Sais instead of two, the third Sai being kept hidden in reserve in the belt on the the backside of the body. This is particularly useful considering that a thrown Sai is usually aimed at the feet. When in times past an Okinawan fighter aimed the point of his Sai at an opponent's foot, he usually managed to pin this to the ground, the ensuing pain causing his opponent to be put out of action long enough to bring him quickly under control. The weapon was so effective that it could be put into use not only against wooden weapons but also against steel weapons such as swords.

Tetsuhiro Hokama, a throwing technique

ETIQUETTE

Re (Bow)

Yoi (Prepare)

Haraki Uke
(Cross Block)

Hajime (Ready, Starting Position)

Naore (Separating)

Finishing (Bow)

B SPECIAL PART:
TECHNIQUES AND FORMS

1. BASIC TECHNIQUES I

A person who has not learned the Way of truth, be it the truth according to Buddha or be it the truth of earthly reason, will consider his own truth to be right and believe in it.

Miyamoto Musashi, A Book of Five Rings

STANCES (Dachi)

Heiko Dachi (Natural Stance I) Feet parallel, shoulder-width apart

Soto Hachiji Dachi (Natural Stance II) Feet turned slightly outwards, shoulder-width apa

a

b

Heisoku Dachi (Ready Stance I)

a

b

Musubi Dachi (Ready Stance II)

Zenkutsu Dachi (Forward Stance)

Gyaku (or Okinawa) **Zenkutsu Dachi** (Rear Defensive Stance)

Kokutsu Dachi (Back Stance)

Nekoashi Dachi (Cat Stance)

Sanchin Dachi (Inner Tension Stance)

Sochin (Fudo) **Dachi** (Outer Tension Stance)

Kiba (Naifanchi) **Dachi** (Horse Stance)

Shiko Dachi (Straddle Stance)

Uchi Hachiji Dachi (Inverse Open Stance)

Rei No Ji Dachi (V-Stance)

a

b

Sagi Ashi (Shirasagiashi) **Dachi** (Crane Stance)

a

b

Kousa Dachi (Cross Stance)

Blocks (Uke)

Jodan Uke (short)

Jodan Uke (long)

a

b

Uchi Uke (short)

a

b

Uchi Uke (long)

Soto Uke (short)

Gedan Uke (short)

Gedan Uke (long)

Ippondachi Gedan Uke

Double Blocks

a

b

Jodan Hiraki Uke (Cross Block) in Honte Mochi

a

b

Gedan Hiraki Uke (Cross Block)

Hiraki Yoko Uke (Cross Block) in Gyaku Mochi

Cross Block (Hiraki Uke) in Gyakute Toko (Jodan, Chudan, Gedan)

Cross Block (Hiraki Uke) in Gyakute Toku

Chudan Morote Uke (short)

Chudan Morote Uke (long)

Gedan Morote Uke (short)

Gedan Morote Uke (long)

Strikes (Uchi)

Downwards Strike Uchiotosu, Uchi Otoshi

Kaeshi Uchi (from outer position)

Kaeshi Uchi (from inner position)

Jodan (Otoshi) Uchi

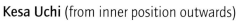

Kesa Uchi (from inner position outwards)

Kesa Uchi (from outer position inwards)

Age Uchi

Soto Uchi

Chudan Yoko Uchi

Gedan Yoko Uchi

Mawashi Uchi

Uraken Uchi

Double Strikes

Morote Soto Uchi

Morote Yoko Uchi

Morote Kesa Uchi

Thrusts (Tsuki)

a   b

Thrusts Tsuku Tsuki
As with Karate, Tsukis can be executed in Oi or Gyaku version

Double techniques

a   b

Morote Tsuki

Yama Tsuki

Other techniques are also similar to Karate application.

Mawashi Tsuki

LUNGE PUNCH (Nuki Tsuki)

Nuki Tsuki free

Nuki Tsuki guided

Jabs can be carried out either with the long end (Saki) or with the short ends (Tsume). There are also many double techniques at various levels.

a

b

Morote Nuki Tsuki

a

b

Yama Nuki Tsuki

Mawashi Nuki Tsuki

Hooks (Hikkakeri)

Hikkakeri are techniques which can be used for attacking vital points. They can also be used for hooking or locking a weapon, a leg or a wrist or arm. When deflecting a weapon, for example, the attack is aimed at the nearest hand. This causes extreme pain, so that the opponent is no longer able to wield his own weapon. The following are a few examples of hooking or locking techniques.

Hooking a weapon

Hooking out of Age Uke, for example, slide down the stick and attack thumb

Hooking through Uchi Uke, for example, lowering and deflecting the stick with pressure on index finger

Hooking out of Harai Uke	Hooking out of Nagashi	Uke or out of Morote Uke

Again, pressure is applied to the opponent's fingers

Out of Gyaku Toku (long hold technique)

Hooking

Attack on thumb

Hooking from outwards	or from inwards	Double technique, again, attack aimed at fingers

Hiraki Uke (short)

Hiraki Uke (short)

The Sais are hooked, so that the opponent's stick is locked and kept under control

Hiraki Uke (long)

deflection inwards

Hooking the sticks and countering (Otoshi Uchi, Otoshi Kiri, this technique is comparable to Hira Basami with bare hands). The combinations follow one another very quickly, so that the opponent has only little chance of countering the Sai.

Locking the Wrist

Locking the Foot

This technique makes it easy to attack known vital/Kyusho points so that leverage can be achieved with little effort. The Sai's pointed ends are ideal for effectively reaching sensitive Kyusho points.

Special Techniques

Hijate

Age Hijate

Yoko Hijate

Mawashi Hijate

Otoshi Hijate

Ushiro Hijate

Throws and Leverage (selected examples)

a

b

c

Soto Tenkai Nage

Leverage of the leg and throw

Ude Kujiki Osae

2. BASIC TECHNIQUES II

The bearing of a warrior...
An imposing bearing entails not turning your face to the earth, nor to heaven, nor side-
ways, nor should it be otherwise distorted...

Miyamoto Musashi, A Book of Five Rings

BASIC TECHNIQUES II

These include advanced techniques which should be practiced both to the left and to the right and which should also be executed in corresponding (Oi) and opposing (Gyaku) positions. We have also shown advanced techniques for defense and attack. There are simple combinations to be practiced which encourage the development of fluid movement with multiple techniques. It is important that these combinations be carried out not only in one direction (forwards and backwards), but also in other varying directions and that they be practiced repeatedly. Backwards movements are practiced mainly in the Kokotsu and Nekoashi stances, which can be done in simple set Kata diagrams. Several typical techniques and combinations are shown as follows. Once again we need to stress the importance of intensively training the use of the hips.

Combinations

1. Oi Tsuki   Ura Uchi   Harai Uke   Gyaku Tsuki

2. Ura Kesa Uchi   Harai Uke   Gyaku Tsuki

3. Oi Tsuki   Gedan Nuki Tsuki   Chudan Nuki Tsuki   Harai Uke

4. Kesa Uchi   Kaeshi Uchi   Harai Uke

5. Uchi Uke   Ura Uchi   Yoko Hijate   Gyuaku Tsuki

1.

Oi Tsuki

Ura Uchi

Harai Uke

Gyaku Tsuki

2.

Ura Kesa Uchi

Harai Uke

Gyaku Tsuki

3.

Oi Tsuki

Gedan Nuki Tsuki

Chudan Nuki Tsuki

Harai Uke

4.

Kesa Uchi

Kaeshi Uchi

Harai Uke

5.

Uchi Uke

Ura Uchi

Yoko Hijate

Gyuaku Tsuki

3. SPECIAL TECHNIQUES WITH PARTNER III

To evaluate the meaning of a weapon, do it this way:
The use of a weapon is dependent upon the given situation, in accordance
with the moment.

Miyamoto Musashi, A Book of Five Rings

Basic Kumite with Partner

T he fundamental content of advanced basics is the movement complexity of various combinations which demand a lot of practice arising from Basic Techniques I and II. It is imperative that these combinations be mastered to both the left and to the right. It is essential to be capable of moving in any direction in order to find the most practical movement for attack and defense. The following shows exercises suitable for advanced combinations and techniques. Repeated practice, perfection of physical dynamics, effective use of Sai acceleration, use of the hips, precise stances and finding the correct center of gravity are essential to achieve optimal technical use of leverage, acceleration and a feeling for distance. It is quite useful to work with the Sai against the Bo as this develops a finer feeling for distance. It also entails less chance of injury on both sides (with Uke and Tori), an important point as starting skills are not yet usually all that well-developed. The Sai is a dangerous weapon and can cause serious injury – please take care when practicing with it.

Basic Kumite with Partner

Sai against Bo

Attack with Bo	Defense	Counter
1. Nuki Tsuki	Nagashi Uchi	Gyaku Nuki Tsuki
2. Yoko Uchi	Nagashi Soto Uke	Nuki Tsuki
3. Gedan uchi	Harai Uke	Gyaku Tsuki
4. Shomen Uchi	Hiraki Uke	Shomen Uchi
5. Age Uchi	Hiraki Uke	Hiraki Uchi
6. Yoko Uchi	Uchi Uke	Yoko Uchi
7. Ura uchi	Harai Uke	Nuki Tsuki
8. Yoko Uchi	Morote Uke	Kesa Uchi
9. Shomen Uchi	Nagashi Uke	Yoko Uchi
10. Yoko Uchi	Morote Hikkakeri	Oi Tsuki

Sai against Bo (Etiquette)

Ready stance Musubi Dachi

Re

Yoi

Ready stance	Attack with Bo/Defense	Counter

1.

Hajime (fighting stance)	Nuki Tsuki/Nagashi Uchi	Gyaku Nuki Tsuki

2.

Synchronized defense and counter

Hajime

Yoko Uchi/Nagashi Soto Uke
Nuki Tsuki

3.

Hajime	Gedan Uchi/Harai Uke	Gyaku Tsuki

4. Ready stance

Hajime

Attack with Bo/Defense

Shomen Uchi/Hiraki Uke

Counter

Shomen Uchi

5. Ready stance

Hajime

Attack with Bo/Defense

Age Uchi/Hiraki Uke

Counter

Hiraki Uchi

6. Ready stance

Hajime

Attack with Bo/Defense

Yoko Uchi /Uchi Uke

Counter

Yoko Uchi /Uchi Uke

7. Ready stance

Hajime

Attack with Bo/Defense

Ura Uchi/Harai Uke

Counter

Nuki Tsuki

8. Ready stance

Hajime

Attack with Bo/Defense

Yoko Uchi/Morote Uke

Counter

Kesa Uchi

9. Ready stance

Hajime

Attack with Bo/Defense

Shomen Uchi/Nagashi Uke

Counter

Yoko Uchi

10. Ready stance

Hajime

Attack with Bo/Defense

Yoko Uchi/Morote Hikkakeri

Counter

Oi Tsuki

4. THE SAI KATA (FORMS)

Everything possesses its own rhythm, but it is in the martial arts especially that rhythm cannot be achieved without constant practice.

Miyamoto Musashi, A Book of Five Rings

The Sai Kata (Forms)

I t is difficult to determine the origin of the various Katas. In some cases they reflect the name of the person who created them, in others they are named after the region or island where they developed. This is the case with the Kata Tsuken Shitakaku no Sai. Notwithstanding the fact that there is also a Tsuken no Kon, or Tsuken Bo (long stick Kata), the various Katas differ considerably according to their school of origin. Although Tsuken is an island on the Ryu Kyu archipelago, the name of origin has been added, so that Tsuken Oyakata in fact means Administrator of Tsuken Island. Many Budo enthusiasts have given a good deal of thought to the origin of various names and have accordingly done a substantial amount of research. The language barrier alone, however, means that a European doing research on origins is going to come up against a lot of obstacles. The peculiarities of actually giving something a name are in some cases only known to insiders, for example with the Kata Maezato no Tekko or Maezato no Kun. According to Sensei Tetsuhiro Hokama, Maezato was the name commonly used for Taira Shinken (1897-1970). This is different to the Bo Katas Ufugusuku no Kun and Oshiro no Kun, for which there are varying, yet related versions. Once again Sensei Hokama was able to provide the information that Ufugusuku (his grandfather's neighbor), was commonly called Oshiro. Here we are dealing with Bo Katas which in themselves differ. A lot of Katas were at some stage changed, either deliberately or otherwise, so that Soken Hohan (1891-1982) probably passed on the already modified Bo Kata Tsuken no Bo To Taira Shinken without revealing its original application. There are most certainly many such similar cases in the history of Karate and Kobudo, which can only be reconstructed either with great difficulty or not at all. The various Sai Katas also differ in style, for example the Karate and Kobudo schools Ryu Kyu Kobudo, the Yamani Ryu, the Honshi Ryu, the Matyoshi Ryu, the Kenshin Ryu, the Kojo Ryu, the Motobu Ryu, the Okinawa Kempo Karate, the Tesshinkan and the Ufuchiku Ryu, among others.

Chatan Yara no Sai

This is a Kata with technical characteristics which do not appear in the usual Sai Katas. The sequence of movement is unusual, for example Manji Gamae in Kiba Dachi, the progression from Gyaku Tsuki with Zenkutsu Dachi into Oi Tsuki with Nekoashi Dachi. The Kata is full of dynamic strength and should ideally be forcefully executed. It is particularly striking that it can be done without weapons and allows for an excellent Bunkai with bare hands. Its origins go back to Chatan Yara (1740-1812).

He was taught by Kushanku (an Envoy of the Chinese Emperor), who was living in Kume and was influenced by the Chinese martial arts expert Wang Chung-Yoh. Kushanku created the Kata Kushanku (later changed in Shotokan and known as Kanku Dai). Kushanku came to Okinawa (Kumemura) with Sappushi in 1756. He taught Sakugawa Kanga and his Uchi Deshi (personal student), who was more knowledgeable of Chinese culture than Sakugawa. Sakugawa significantly moved the emphasis of the Kata Kushanku towards fighting, whereas the Chatan Yara line retained the original character of the Kata with its emphasis on health training (Tai Chi elements) and Kyusho (application of vital points). Chatan Yara was a famous Kobujutsu expert who was alive during the reign of King Sho Buko. His Sai Kata is still well-known up to the present time, as is his Karate Kata Chatan Yara no Kusanku. He was in all probability born in Shuri, and later sailed per government order with the royal troops to Yomitan Magiri. At some stage he went to Yara and became known as Yara von Chatan.

Calligraphy by T. Hokama
Chatan Yara no Sai

Tetsuhiro Hokama in the Kata
Yara no Sai

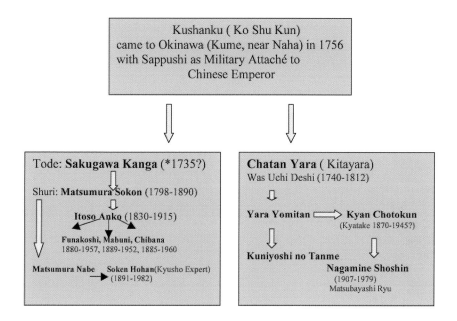

Kushanku (Ko Shu Kun)
came to Okinawa (Kume, near Naha) in 1756
with Sappushi as Military Attaché to
Chinese Emperor

Tode: **Sakugawa Kanga** (*1735?)

Shuri: **Matsumura Sokon** (1798-1890)

Itoso Anko (1830-1915)

Funakoshi, Mabuni, Chibana
1880-1957, 1889-1952, 1885-1960

Matsumura Nabe   **Soken Hohan**(Kyusho Expert)
(1891-1982)

Chatan Yara (Kitayara)
Was Uchi Deshi (1740-1812)

Yara Yomitan ⟹ **Kyan Chotokun**
(Kyatake 1870-1945?)

Kuniyoshi no Tanme
Nagamine Shoshin
(1907-1979)
Matsubayashi Ryu

Chatan Yara and the origin of several Okinawa Karate and Kobudo Masters up to the present day

Chikin (Tsuken) Shitahaku no Sai

This is a long Kata which is not difficult to learn as its combinations are repeated several times in varying sequences. It contains a lot of interesting and differing techniques. Repeating the sequences does, however, contain the temptation to reel them off too automatically, so it is most important not to fall into this trap. It is one of the more advanced Katas.

According to Mitsugu, it is possible that this Kata was developed by a Kobudo expert called Sai Taku (1644-1724), who travelled to China as a young man but was forced to return at an early stage due to ill health. He took on several official contracts and travelled to China on many occasions in government service. In 1682 he took on the position as General Administrator for the Chinese Emperor in Kumemura. He was Adminstrator for the Island of Tsuken; his first name was apparently Shitahaku, so that he was known as Shitahaku of Tsuken (Mitsugu Matsuda: The Ryukyuan Government Scholarship Students to China, 1392-1868: Based on a Short Essay by Nakahara Zench 363; 1962. p. 295. Monumenta Nipponica, Vol. 21: 3/4 (1966).

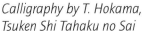

Calligraphy by T. Hokama, Tsuken Shi Tahaku no Sai   *Tetsuhiro Hokama in Maso Gamae, Sagiashi Dachi*

Hamahiga no Sai

Hamahiga no Sai is a typical and very demanding Okinawan Kata, the movements of which show a clear relationship to the Kata Tsuken Shitahaku. Hamahiga and Tsuken Shitahaku were practiced in Ryu Kyu Kobujutsu, other versions exist in other schools, as with Sensei Hokama. Hamahiga no Sai originates from the Hamahiga Island, near and to the east of the main island Okinawa in the Pacific. It was settled relatively late, and consists of the townships of Hama and Higa. The special Katas of this island were probably influenced by the old Matsu Higa system (1647-1721) and by the island's old weaponry culture. Here you can still find traces of the influence of the Shorei Ryu. The name Hama Higa Pechin (Pechin = public servant) is obviously connected to the development of the Kata. This island was also the origin of the armed Katas Hamahiga no Tonfa and Hamahiga no Kama.

Calligraphy by T. Hokama
Hamahiga no Sai

Tetsuhiro Hokama with the Kata
Hamahiga no Sai

AKAMINE NO SAI

The Akamine no Sai Kata is a relatively short Kata with an unusual pattern of steps (Embusen). Its execution varies, depending on the style it is carried out in, for example Shorin Ryu. The name Akamine Eisuke (1925-1999) is associated with this Kata. He studied under Higa Seiichiro, a Master of Yamanni Ryu, and later (from 1959) under Taira Shinken, the founder of Ryukyu Kobudo Hozon Shinkokai. Taira Shinken recorded a large number of armed Katas in book form, which was unique in that up until that time information had always been passed down by word of mouth. Akamine is accredited with having created the Akamine no Sai Kata.

Chiara no Sai

Matayoshi Kobudo has several versions, which can primarily be seen as training Katas. The Chiara no Sai Shodan is also practiced in Shorin Ryu. No further information on its origin is available to date. It is a simple basic Kata for beginners which is easy to learn and contains the most important techniques.

Chibana no Sai

According to Tetsuhiro Hokama this Kata originates from Chibana Castle, which now only exists as a ruin on Okinawa. The Kata was most probably created by the royal family of Chibana. Chibana no Sai contains typical elements of the Naha Te, as well as the Shuri Te. It is relatively simple and follows a pattern (Embusen) which is easy to comprehend. Evasive leg movements are characteristic, for example for countering sweeping movements or attack by an opponent's stick. This Kata can be carried out with two or three Sais.

Calligraphy by T. Hokama
Chibana no Sai

Tetsuhiro Hokama in the first movement of
Chibana no Sai

It is important to take several basic principles into consideration when carrying out the Kata. Katas are not ballet. They should be executed in such a manner that the Bunkai (purpose) is clearly obvious. A Kata lacks life if there is no visible purpose. Even though one can fine-tune the exact stances such as Kokutsu Dachi, Sagiashi Dachi etc., dynamics remain the decisive factor. The various basic positions are worked through in natural movement. The stances themselves are not the purpose of a Kata but serve only as an aid to movement.

Patrick McCarthy has aptly summarized the essential principles of the Kata in his book "Ancient Okinawan Martial Arts" as follows:

Yoi no Kishin	mental preparation
Inyo	understanding cause and effect
Go no Sen, Sen no Sen and Sen	principles of the initiative
Mai	a feeling for correct distance (Mai) and Tai Sabaki
Tai no Shinshuku	tension and relaxation (muscles, movement)
Chikara no Kyojaku	the correct use of strength in every technique
Kiai-jutsu	the correct use of flow of power (Ki)
Waza no Kankyu	speed and rhythm of a technique
Ju no Ri	the principle of calm and endurance under a volley of attack
Kokyu	synchronizing breathing according to tension and relaxation
Bunkai	recognizing purpose
Zanshin	constant readiness for fight (attentiveness)
Seishi o Choetzu	suppression of thoughts of life or death

The following illustrations of traditional Katas show a possible interpretation of movement sequences and are in no way binding.

Basically all Katas are suitable for practicing the basic techniques. Sometimes it is useful for training purposes to restrict oneself to single sequences. The most important factors for performing Katas are correct rhythm, good hip rotation and precision in technique. It is essential to visualize the purpose (Bunkai) when demonstrating, otherwise the Kata will appear to be dull and without meaning.

Enjoy your training.

SAI KATA

Chiara no Sai Shodan

Chibana no Sai

Chatan Yara no Sai

Tsuken Shitakaku no Sai

Hamahiga no Sai

Akamine no Sai

CHIARA NO SAI SHODAN

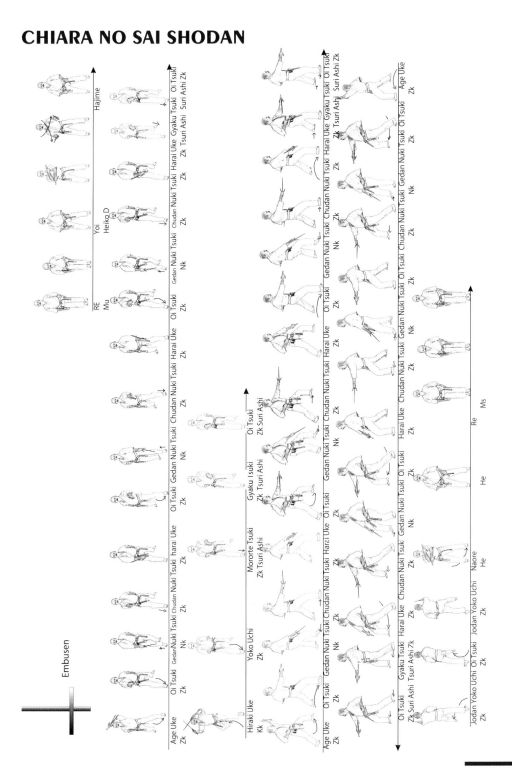

CHIBANA NO SAI

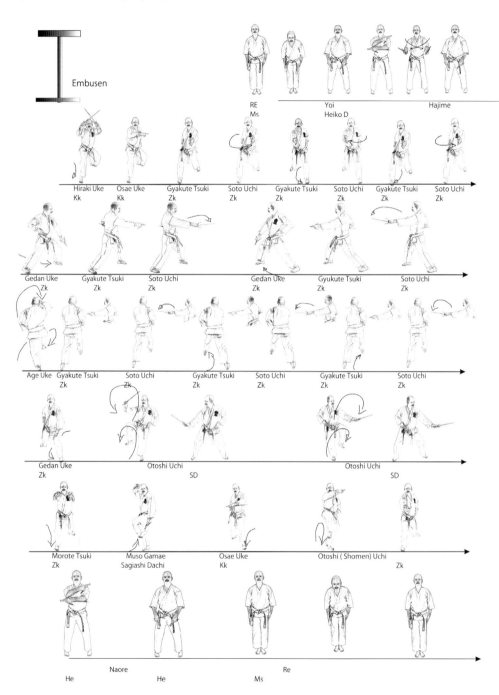

Embusen

RE
Ms

Yoi
Heiko D

Hajime

Hiraki Uke	Osae Uke	Gyakute Tsuki	Soto Uchi	Gyakute Tsuki	Soto Uchi	Gyakute Tsuki	Soto Uchi
Kk	Kk	Zk	Zk	Zk	Zk	Zk	Zk

Gedan Uke	Gyakute Tsuki	Soto Uchi	Gedan Uke	Gyukute Tsuki	Soto Uchi
Zk	Zk	Zk	Zk	Zk	Zk

Age Uke	Gyakute Tsuki	Soto Uchi	Gyakute Tsuki	Soto Uchi	Gyakute Tsuki	Soto Uchi
	Zk	Zk	Zk	Zk	Zk	Zk

Gedan Uke		Otoshi Uchi			Otoshi Uchi	
Zk			SD			SD

Morote Tsuki	Muso Gamae	Osae Uke	Otoshi (Shomen) Uchi	
Zk	Sagiashi Dachi	Kk		Zk

	Naore			Re	
He		He		Ms	

CHATAN YARA NO SAI

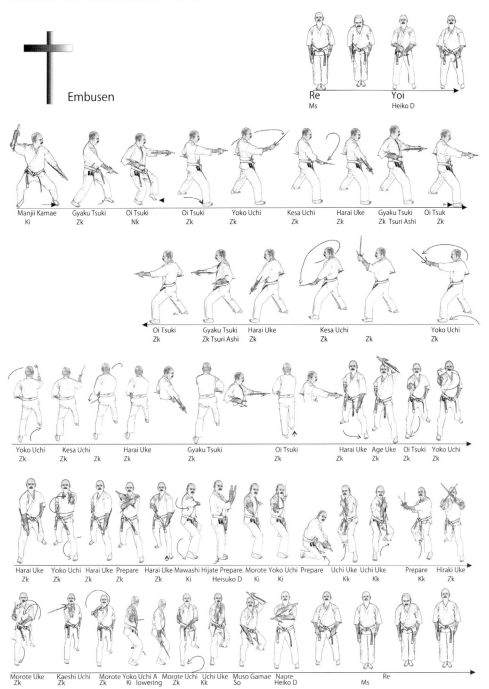

Embusen

Re	Yoi
Ms	Heiko D

Manjii Kamae Ki	Gyaku Tsuki Zk	Oi Tsuki Nk	Oi Tsuki Zk	Yoko Uchi Zk	Kesa Uchi Zk	Harai Uke Zk	Gyaku Tsuki Zk Tsuri Ashi	Oi Tsuk Zk

Oi Tsuki Zk	Gyaku Tsuki Zk Tsuri Ashi	Harai Uke Zk	Kesa Uchi Zk		Yoko Uchi Zk

Yoko Uchi Zk	Kesa Uchi Zk	Harai Uke Zk	Gyaku Tsuki Zk	Oi Tsuki Zk	Harai Uke Zk	Age Uke Zk	Oi Tsuki Zk	Yoko Uchi Zk

Harai Uke Zk	Yoko Uchi Zk	Harai Uke Zk	Prepare Zk	Harai Uke Zk	Mawashi Hijate Ki	Prepare. Heisuko D	Morote Yoko Uchi Ki	Prepare Ki	Uchi Uke Kk	Uchi Uke Kk	Prepare Kk	Hiraki Uke Zk

Morote Uke Zk	Kaeshi Uchi Zk	Morote Zk	Yoko Uchi A Ki lowering	Morote Uchi Zk	Uchi Uke Kk	Muso Gamae So	Naore Heiko D	Re	
								Ms	

119

TSUKEN SHITAHAKU NO SAI (PART I)

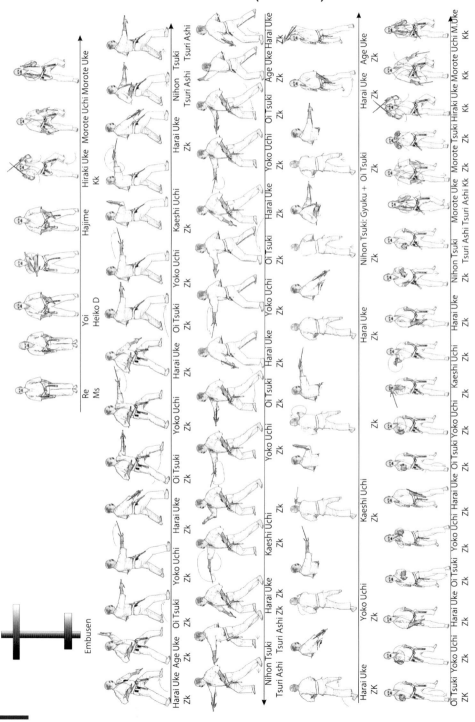

TSUKEN SHITAHAKU NO SAI (PART II)

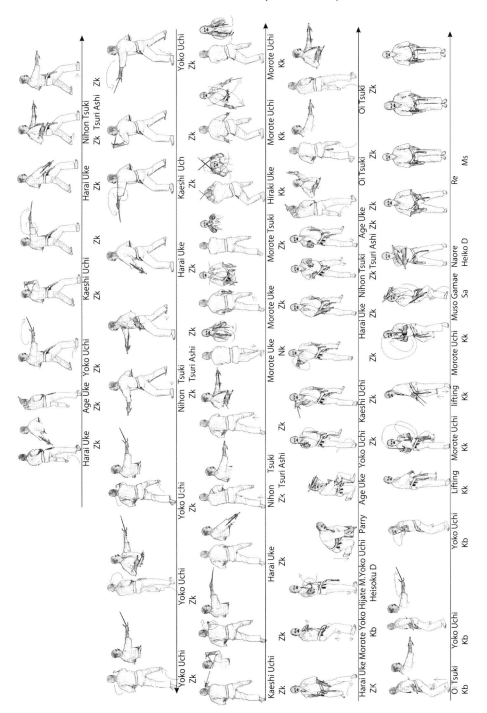

HAMAHIGA NO SAI (PART I)

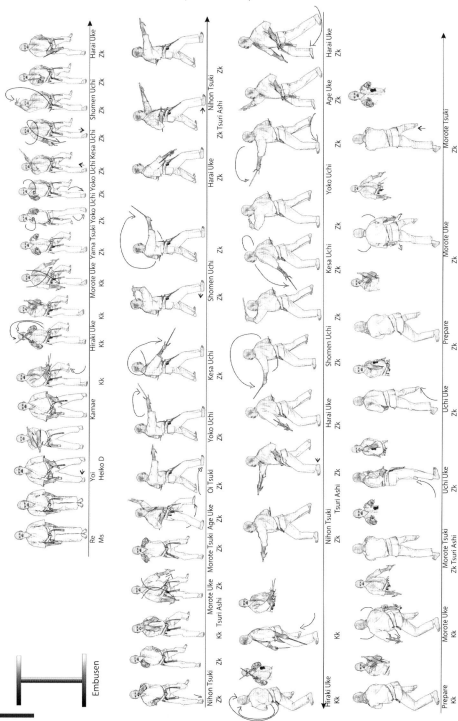

HAMAHIGA NO SAI (PART II)

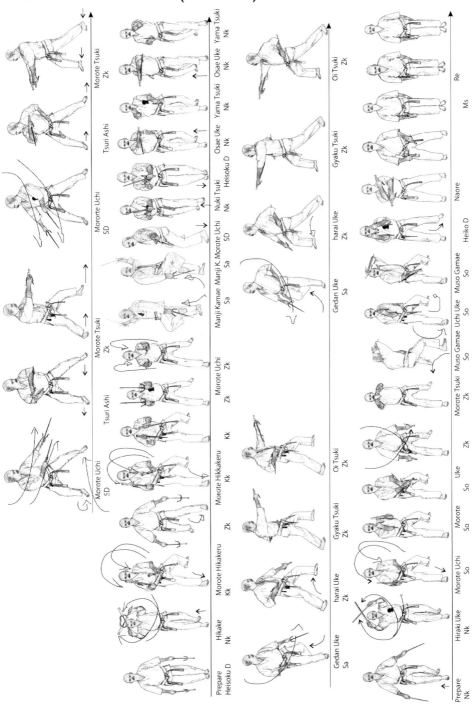

AKAMINE NO SAI

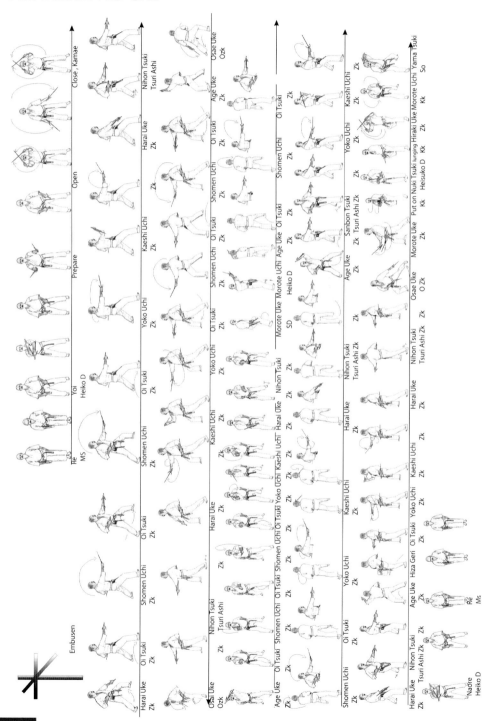

CLOSING REMARKS

Kobudo (formerly called Kobu-Jutsu) contains a great number of different weapons. Whereas a great number of katas could be passed on for Bo-Jutsu, the same thing has only been achieved for different weapons in a restricted way. In addition to martial arts without weapons (Karate, Aikido, Jujutsu and others) Kobudo is being practiced at almost every school. As practicing with weapons often demands total concentration, it is advisable, especially for beginners, to start their training program with weapons and to continue without weapons afterwards. As a matter of principle, before the students can be introduced to the Kobudo techniques, they should have the important basic techniques of the martial arts without weapons under control. As a rule, the long stick (Bo) is the basic weapon for Kobudo. The other weapons, such as Tonfa, Nunchaku, Sai and Kama, make higher demands on the students. That does not only apply to motions but also to the risk of injury. However, every experienced martial arts fighter knows that practicing with weapons serves to improve and to support the techniques of martial arts without weapons, as for example the sense of motions in karate. The techniques of martial arts with empty hands become more exact and quick. Insofar, Kobudo is not only a welcome supplement but even more an essential enlargement of the martial arts practiced so far. On the one hand, the main task of future great masters will be to preserve the knowledge about the martial arts and its deep-rooted traditions and on the other hand, to further develop different techniques of the weapons.

The IMAF-Kokusai Budoin (International Martial Art Federation) is a non-profit organization looking for different Budo disciplines. It was founded after World War II in 1952. In February 1952 the first Budo Exhibition was presented in the Hibiya Park in Tokyo. The first Budo demonstration was planned in 1951 by K. Mifune K. Ito and S. Sato (Judo), H. Nakayama and H. Takano (Kendo), H. Otsuka (Karate), K. Wake and S. Kiyura. Prince Tsunenori Kaya was elected the first president of the National Japan Health Association, the first name of the IMAF. The current president is Yasuhisa Tokugawa, one member of the ancient Tokugawa Dynasty, a family of Shoguns who ruled in Japan in peace for nearly 300 years. The IMAF has seven departments: Judo, Kendo, Karatedo, Iaido, Aikido, Nihon Jujutsu and Kobudo. In these departments there are different styles of martial arts. The IMAF is inaugurated by the family of the Tenno to give high ranks in all kinds of Budo art and to give titles of honor (Renshi, Kyoshi, Hanshi, and Mejin). Since its foundation, the aim of the IMAF Kokusai Budoin has been to make

Japanese Martial Arts popular throughout the whole world and to seek further development. The vision is that with the help of Budo arts all people in the world learn how to live in harmony. It wants to help them reach peace and understanding between different nations. The IMAF Kokusai Budoin has members in more than 50 nations; 17 branch directors are responsible for international exchange. The IMAF has friendly relations with other Budo organizations; some leaders are honored members of the IMAF.

I am particularly grateful to my students and my two sons for their support in planning the book and their assistance during the photo sessions. Their names are listed in the acknowledgments that follow the text. Thanks also to my wife Elvira for her patience and for taking the numerous photos. Thanks to Mrs. Judy Keenan for the English translation of the German original.

Lutz Kogel
3ʳᵈ DAN Karate

Marc Kogel
3ʳᵈ DAN Karate, 1ᵗʰ DAN Kobudo

Klaus Parensen
1ˢᵗ DAN Karate

Günay Aidincioglon
1ˢᵗ DAN Karate

LITERATURE

1. Clavell J. (1988). *Sunzi*, Die Kunst des Krieges. München: DroemerscheVerl. Anstalt, ThKnaur Nachf.
2. Demura F. (1974). *Sai, Karate Weapon of Self-defense*. Santa Clarita, California: Ohara Publ Inc.
3. Habersetzer R. (2006). *Kobudo-1, Bo, Sai*. Chemnitz: Palisander Verlag.
4. Habersetzer R. (2007). *Kobudo-2, Nunchaku, Tonfa, Polizei-Tonfa*. Chemnitz: Palisander Verlag.
5. Hokama T. (2006). *100 Masters of Okinawan Karate*. Japan: Ozato Print Co. Okinawa.
6. Hokama T. (2007). *Timeline of Karate History*. Japan: Ozato Print Co.Okinawa
7. Inoe M. (1987). *Bo, Sai, Tonfa and Nunchaku, ancient Martial Art of the Ryu Kyu Islands*. Tokyo: Seitosho Co. Ltd.
8. Kogel H. (2005). *Kobudo-Bo-Jutsu, Technique – Training – Katas*. Aachen: Meyer und Meyer Verl.
10. Kim R. (1985). *Kobudo, Okinawan Weapons of Hama Higa*. Hamilton, Ontario Canada: Masters Publication.
11. Lind W. (1977). *Okinawa Karate*. Berlin: Sportverlag Berlin GmbH
12. Musashi, M. (1994). *Fünf Ringe*. München: Droemersche Verlagsanstalt Th.Knaur Nachf.
13. McCarthy. (1999) *Ancient Okinawan Martial Arts*. Bosto, Rutland VT, Tokyo: Tuttle Publishing.
14. McCarthy P. (1987). *Classic Kata of Okinawan Karate*. Santa Clarita, California: Ohara Publ.Inc.
15. Shinken T. (2004). *Encyclopedia of Okinawan Weapons*. Hamilton, Ontario Canada: Masters Pulication.
16. Yamamoto T. (2000). *Hagakure, der Weg des Samurai*. München: Piper Verl. München.

PHOTO & ILLUSTRATIONS CREDITS

Cover Photo and
Inside Photos: Helmut Kogel
Cover Design: Jens Vogelsang

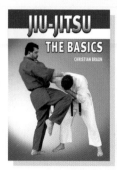
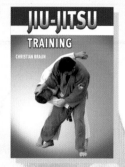

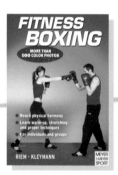

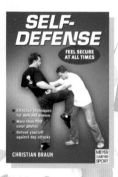